To A
GoD

Twelve Steps to your Healing is a

blessing & blessen
in today & always.
Shaela

Twelve Steps to Your Healing
By Sheila R. McKeithen

ISBN: 978-0692309261

Cover Design by Sharon Deheney Walker.
sharon@ssensedesigns.com

Dedication

To the Spirit of the Almighty Healer that resides in every soul, awaiting recognition of Its eternal presence and everlasting power.

To the Reverend Dr. Johnnie M. Colemon, Founder and President Emerita of the Universal Foundation for Better Living Inc., who through her life example and spiritual teachings inspired me to "let healing through."

To the Reverend Dr. Mary A. Tumpkin, who challenged me to live true to the principles that Rev. Colemon taught us and encouraged me through my healing journey.

To every student who, subsequent to hearing my testimony of healing, asked me to put pen to paper and share with a broader audience the steps to healing.

In memory of Joseph E. Robinson, whose last words to me were, "What are the steps to healing?"

In memory of Miss Reid, a stranger, who practiced the steps in this book while the writings were in the infancy stage and shared that her application of the steps in her life brought her the relief she sought.

Table of Contents

Steps

A Word from the Author

The information in this book is based on my personal experiences and interactions with persons with whom I have shared my healing testimony. Any resemblance or similarity to other people's experiences is purely coincidental.

This book makes no medical predictions, diagnoses, or prognoses. It is intended for persons who wish to work through their life circumstances from the level of the soul. The decision to seek or not to seek psychiatric, medical, or holistic healing assistance of any kind, from any individual or entity in the universe, is left completely up to the individual.

I wish to acknowledge Sharon Deheney Walker of S'sense Designs, a wonderful friend who designed, formatted, and provided valuable input to make this book available to a wider audience.

I also wish to acknowledge Tawnicia Ferguson Rowan, Founder and CEO of Well-Written Words, LLC, for editing this book in a way that kept its "spiritual flavor" intact.

Last, but not least, I thank you, dear reader, for holding the healing vision for our world and for yourself.

An Invitation

This book invites you into a new way of thinking about yourself. You are special. Your realization of the biblical truths contained in this book are sure to have a positive effect on you as you take your journey into healing.

I have found that we have a tendency to carry unnecessary baggage, emotional and otherwise, as we travel in life. That baggage weighs us down and generally interferes with our ability to live happier and healthier lives. Heavy baggage such as unforgiveness, self-doubt, fear, frustration, resentment, anger, and worry takes its toll on us. Our bodies send us signals indicating that it is time to unpack, to travel lighter so that we can journey farther in life. Unfortunately, in our busyness, we tend to ignore the cues and clues that are being sent to us on a daily basis. Sometimes we don't acknowledge the signs until we are flat on our backs, having fallen under the pressure of the load we bear.

This book offers you the opportunity to change the unhealthy patterns that you have created for yourself. It invites you to step into a new way of thinking about yourself and the lifestyle you have chosen. Are your daily choices working for you or against you? Are your thoughts and feelings about what others did or did not do helping you fulfill your goals, or are they sabotaging your opportunities for success? Are feelings of disappointment, anger, jealousy, and fear eating at your inward parts and causing all kinds of health problems? If you recognize that it is time to make better choices for and about yourself, keep reading this book.

The journey you are about to take is a spiritual one. It will either introduce or re-introduce you to your True self, your spiritual SELF. The spiritual SELF is the aspect of you that can't be fooled by symptoms, diagnoses, or prognoses. It is the You that understands that you are more than you've expressed up until this moment. It knows only the best for you and supports you in your desire to be whole. It knows that God loves you and always will love you. It also knows that spiritually speaking, health is your birthright, a gift from God that you can claim beginning now.

This book offers you the opportunity to take a spiritual adventure in faith. This adventure is not about placing blame on others. Instead, it is designed to help you become very clear that, as a spiritual being, you can choose to unpack the baggage of negativity and travel light through life as you embrace your true identity as a child of God. What I know for sure is that when you are clear about who you are as a spiritual being, that knowledge alone will open the way for the errors of the past, be they yours or another's, to be purged so that they are no longer a hindrance to you. It is time for you to live a healthier, happier, and more successful life. Only you can decide to accept this invitation. If your decision is "Yes," let's begin.

The Beginning

In 1985, I was a physically fit officer of the law with dreams of one day becoming an attorney. In late December, I noticed that I did not feel fit at all, only weak. I ventured to the shopping mall, purchased workout gear, and joined a gym, only to find myself on the floor gasping for breath before the end of the aerobics session. Something was definitely wrong. So, off to the doctor I went. He ordered me to go to the hospital immediately. The prognosis: I had less than 6 days to live. I was in my twenties and had not yet learned to live, so I did not understand why I had to die. I had only just begun to achieve some of my dreams. During my three-year journey into healing, I was also told that my leg would be amputated, but this was quickly dismissed when a doctor assured me, "We will get through this." I was actually ordered to leave the hospital because I was considered too much of a risk, but I learned to walk again after months of being unable to do so.

Discouragement—I encountered it. Pity—I joined many of its parties. Quit—I entertained it, until I changed my mind.

As I speak to audiences around the world, people ask me again and again: "Where do I start?" "How can I follow up with you?" "Where is your book so that I can read it?"

These questions are among many of the reasons that I have written this book. I've identified twelve steps that have helped me to heal and to stay well. Through this book, I am sharing these twelve steps with you. These steps have nothing to do with the physical modalities you may choose to assist you in your healing journey. In fact, the twelve steps outlined in this book can be utilized along with your medical care and other methodologies that you find useful. No matter where you are in your healing journey, you are invited to use this book as often as you choose. I have found that we often saturate our minds and hearts with our challenges, and the result is fear. So why can't we saturate our minds and hearts with spiritual Truth and see what happens? Again, the invitation is extended. You must decide to accept it.

A Testimony

In 2012, a woman whom I had never met made a counseling appointment to see me. As I approached her to introduce myself, I noticed that her eyes were yellow in color. I had never encountered anyone with such an issue. After I opened our appointment with prayer, she began to speak. As she spoke, I felt an urge to give her a small pamphlet I had written that contained nine of the twelve scriptures in this book. At that time, I had no commentary or titles, only the scriptures. I gave the pamphlet to her and told her to work with the scriptures in the order in which they were written. She took the pamphlet, and there was no further talk about a subsequent appointment. We said our goodbyes.

Approximately three months later, while extending greetings and hugs in my spiritual community, I hugged a woman who turned to me and asked, "You don't remember me?" After looking very closely at her, I said, "You are the lady with the eyes." She smiled the prettiest smile and said, "Yes, I am." Her eyes twinkled with no signs of yellow, only clear-ness. I then said, "My goodness, what did you do? You look great." She replied, "Remember that little pamphlet you gave to me? It worked." I just hugged her.

I share this testimony because she wanted me to, and to encourage anyone who has read this far to keep going. Finish the book. Work with the ideas presented and let these ideas seep into your being, renewing you and blessing you today and always.

Introduction

Each of the twelve biblical statements discussed in this book is a true statement about you. Read each statement and its explanation again and again. Personalize the statement. Decide what it means for you in your present circumstances. Decide that the course of your life can be changed beginning today as you daily contemplate each statement. Your quest is to fill your mind and heart with these words of Truth so much so that they ooze forth in your life and affairs in visible ways.

My prayer for you is that the inspiration that flows from your heart as you embrace each statement will open up the healing rivers within you and reveal your birthright of wholeness, health, and success.

Read these Bible truths as often as possible. Stand on them and refuse to be moved. "...stand firm, and see the deliverance that the Lord will accomplish for you today...." Exodus 14:13

Twelve Steps to your Healing

Step One

Claim Your Inheritance

"We are from God ... ." I John 4:6

The sooner you realize your true identity as a child of God, the quicker healing in mind, body, and affairs is demonstrated. There is no greater Truth than that you must Know Who You Are. Know at the core of your being that as a child of God, your inheritance is wholeness. Because this is so, you have a right to be whole and to witness that wholeness as your reality here and now. As an heir to wholeness, you must stake your claim. Claim wholeness in the face of every appearance.

There is nothing you have done, no choice that you have made, and no circumstance or external factors that can prevent you from claiming your inheritance of wholeness right now. Dare to say: "I CLAIM wholeness now!"

Say and feel these words until you accept them as the truth about yourself.

In the midst of your circumstances, all is not lost. You are a child of God, and God's will for you is wholeness. If you are facing surgery, claim wholeness. When doctors give up and say there is no more they can do, claim wholeness! When you feel lonely and abandoned by those you thought would always be with you, claim wholeness! When debts are high and income low, claim wholeness! Claim your wholeness every day in every way, and wholeness shall be yours. God made you whole. Refuse to accept otherwise.

Affirmation:

God is wholeness. I am from God. I am whole. I claim wholeness now!

Step Two

Accept Your True Nature

*"God created humankind in his image, in the image of
God he created them; male and female he created them.
God blessed them ... ." Genesis 1:27-28*

God is Spirit. If the above scripture
is true, and you are the image and
likeness of God, then you are a spiritual being. Yes, you appear in human form, but
your true essence is spiritual. Spiritual qualities
like love, peace, wholeness, harmony, happiness, and joy are, therefore, a natural part of
your being. They are gifts. God gave them to
you. In order to enjoy the gifts, you must open
the package.

Once you accept that the gifts are yours,
begin to use them. Find ways to be loving
towards yourself and others. Practice peace
because peace begins in you. Choose harmony,
joy, and happiness instead of guilt, shame, and
frustration. Every time you choose to express the

gifts that are within you, you nurture the soul. The soul is then able to expand and grow. The result is happier, healthier experiences in life.

The soul plays an important role in sustaining the physical body. When it is well nourished, the body thrives. When it is not nourished, the body feels the effects.

Another way to nurture the soul is through spiritual practices like prayer, meditation, quiet contemplation, and seeking after the spiritual life. If your soul is spiritually strengthened, it will overcome the challenges it meets. The exercises in this book strengthen the soul. The more you engage in these exercises, the stronger the soul becomes.

If the challenge before you appears to be great, you must exercise the soul consistently. The soul can only deliver back to you what you have invested in it. Invest much and receive much. Invest little and receive little. Love yourself enough to invest in yourself generously.

Love is within you because God is Love. As the image and likeness of God, you can express love, accept love, and give love. In fact, you are love, and you are loved.

Do you believe that God loves you? Yes, YOU! In the face of fault, fear, success, and triumph, the truth is: God loves you. Say these words again and again: "God loves me." Say them until you feel love's vibration taking up residence in your body and in your affairs.

Love is an amazing healer. Invite Divine Love to have Its way in your life. Allow love to navigate you through the conditions that seem so treacherous. Give love permission to be in charge of all that concerns you. Cooperate with love's efforts by speaking loving words; thinking loving thoughts; feeling loving feelings; responding and acting from a space of love. Love will never fail you, if you trust it in all circumstances. Loving feelings, thoughts, words, actions, and reactions will nurture your soul. The soul, in turn, will regenerate your body temple as well as your body of affairs.

Affirmation:

I am made in the image and likeness of God. I lovingly cooperate with my spiritual nature in thought, word, and deed. The love that I am regenerates my body and my affairs.

Step Three

It's All Within You

"For 'In him we live and move and have our being ...
For we too are his offspring.'" Acts 17:28

It is important to remember that you are
always in the presence of the goodness of
God. As a fish is to the sea, so you are to
God. You live, move, and have your being in
God's goodness. This means that you and God
are one. Jesus believed this to be so, and you
must, too.

A fish doesn't ask for water as it swims
in the sea; it is already immersed in the
seawaters. So, too, are you immersed in the
magnificence of God's love, grace, and healing
power. It may not appear to be so, but it is. A
fish doesn't see the water in which it swims,
but it feels the effects of the water. You don't
see the oxygen that you breathe day in and
day out, but you know it is there because you
inhale it. You may not see or even feel the

healing power of God flowing within you, but it is there.

As you read these words, the healing energies are being stirred up within your soul. That is why I suggest that you read the words in this book again and again. The more you read and entertain these ideas, the greater the flow of energy within you will be. Remember, invest much and receive much. Invest little and receive little. Isn't it great to know that you can demand as much of the healing energy as you wish through your concentrated practice of these spiritual truths? Turn off the television or whatever is distracting you from giving these exercises your undivided attention.

Your spiritual inheritance of life, wisdom, power, love, and an abundance of good is available to you right now. If you haven't claimed your inheritance, it passively awaits you. Even if you don't believe that you have an inheritance, it awaits you. Your belief does not change the truth of your spiritual inheritance. Your belief can, however, delay the expression of these gifts in your life.

Delay is not denial. At any time, you can choose to believe that you are doomed, or you can believe that there is a way forward. Whatever you choose will also choose you. I think you will agree that if you choose to believe the worst about yourself and your circumstances, you will likely get the worst possible results. On the other hand, the person who chooses wholeheartedly to expect the best is more likely to succeed than one who chooses to believe that he or she is stuck with no chance of getting unstuck. Do you agree?

The power to choose is yours. As an offspring of God with access to the radiant promises of God, what will you choose for yourself? Will it be health or sickness? Will it be peace or turmoil? Will it be financial stability or financial ruin? Will it be love or hate? Whatever you choose, chooses you and attaches itself to you. Your choices follow you wherever you go. Let's choose wisely.

Affirmation:

I forever live in the presence of God. I choose to express the good in life that God designed just for me. I accept my good right now!

Step Four

Speak the Word of Truth

"God lives in us, and his love is perfected in us."
I John 4:12

Question: "Where is God?"

Answer: "Right where you are as Everywhere
            Present Spirit."

There is no place where you will go and find God absent or missing. Are you in the hospital? God is there. Are you feeling lonely? God is there. Are you in jail? God is there. Wherever you are, God is always with you. God never has and never will abandon you.

God's love lives in you. God's perfect life is your life here and now. God's life is perfect within you and knows no flaws. Its desire is to be more perfect in you so that you may express greater degrees of perfection in all that you do, say, feel, and think. Everything about you exudes

God's perfection. Refuse to let an unfavorable diagnosis or prognosis blind you to the perfection of God that is within you.

Many times, we don't recognize our inner perfection as often as we recognize our flaws and mistakes. When an unfavorable opinion is given to you, see it as an opportunity to awaken the perfection that is resting dormant within you. Call God's perfection within you forth by saying: "Perfect life, come forth. Perfect health, come forth. Divine Energy, come forth." Whatever seems to be lacking in you, call it forth with conviction. Set an appointment time with God, and give your undivided attention to calling forth the latent or dormant healing and restoring power within you. Call it forth from the depths of your being. Bid it to come and work on your behalf.

The amount of time you give to this assignment will be equal to the benefit that you receive. If you can put yourself on a schedule for taking doses of medication, you can put yourself on a schedule for quiet contemplation and meditation. It is never too late to call forth the perfection of God within you. Try it. Set your schedule to suit the results you'd like to see, and then begin.

Affirmation:

I call forth the healing energy within me. I am restored. I am healed. All is well.

Step Five

Become That Which You Already Are

"Be perfect, therefore, as your heavenly Father is perfect." Matthew 5:48

Do you believe that as a child of God you have the right to demand perfection in your body and affairs? Perfection doesn't mean that you will never face seeming problems and challenges or failures in life. However, it does mean that you can meet every problem or challenge with faith.

Do you have faith that all things are working together for good, even if you don't see visible signs of good? Do you have faith that your worst nightmare can become your greatest blessing? Does your faith remind you that even your darkest night can bring joy in the morning? In reality, all you have is your faith in God. Can you trust your faith in God to accomplish its perfect work in your life?

To be perfect is to let God's love, peace, harmony, joy, and generosity flow through you on a daily basis. When you choose to let that happen, there will be no need to judge yourself based on circumstances and facts. You will know that seeming problems come your way to pass out of your way. The more you allow them to pass, refusing to become fixated on them, the quicker they will leave your life.

As you meet and overcome problems, you prove to others that they can do the same. Someone somewhere has her or his eye on you.

Someone somewhere is pulling for you and wants to see you break through. Now, press beyond fear and dismay. There is no need to fear. The Lord your God is with you here and now. Be still and experience it.

Affirmation:

I choose to give my attention to the perfection of God that indwells me. Where I appear weak, God is strong. This circumstance has come to pass, not to last. I let it pass as I rest in the perfection that I am. God in, through, and as me sees me through.

Step Six

Embrace the Power of Love

"...perfect love casts out fear [disease] ... ." I John 4:18

Love is a magnificent healer. When you bring the love that you are to all that you do, fear dissipates. Doubt fades. Worry dissolves. Self-sabotage disintegrates. Envy vanishes. Resentment, shame, and guilt are all exposed as the cowards that they are. Not one of these limiting feeling patterns can survive an encounter with love. Not one.

Your quest is to let love have its way in your life. You cannot afford to let feelings and thoughts of unforgiveness wreck your life. It just isn't worth it. Is it? Your dislike of another person doesn't prevent that person from living the life she or he chooses. The truth of the matter is that your dislikes only affect you. Another's dislike of you affects her or him, not you. Love will always have her way, in her own time, and as she sees fit. If healing is a priority for you, then unforgiveness must be cast aside. The two (unforgiveness and healing) do not keep company with one another.

Choose to make healing a priority in your life. There are ways that you can experience a boost of health and love in your life. How? Try laughing more often. Author Norman Cousins in his book *Anatomy of an Illness* says he laughed himself back to health. Laughter, then, must be good medicine.

What can you do to stir up the healing energy within you? Take note of emotions that slow down or even prevent the circulation of healing energy in your body. Are there any regrets, hatred, or fears lurking within you? If so, release them. They make you a magnetic force for unfavorable conditions that rob you of your inheritance of wholeness.

Begin now to withdraw your attention from toxic emotions. Refuse to speak negative words or entertain unhealthy feelings. When you withdraw your energy and attention from the negative, there is nothing to sustain its existence. Without sustenance, negativity dies. The way is now clear for the positive flow of your healing life energies that willingly aid you in the healing process.

Affirmation:

My priority is love and healing. I choose to love myself and share love with others. I am healed as a result.

Step Seven:

Power to Overcome Fear

"For God hath not given us the spirit of fear[disease];
but [the spirit] of power, and of love [healing] ... ."
II Timothy 1:7 (KJV)

As a spiritual being, you have the power of God at your disposal. Take your place and respond to every suggestion of wrongdoing from a point of power and mastery. When you do, you abandon the victim role. A celebrity once said, "After losing eighty percent of the money I earned, I decided to get up, dust off, and try it again." Guess what? He earned all that was previously lost and more. You, too, can exert your God-given power to choose. In every instance, you can choose to keep going and growing, even if others stop or give up.

There will be many opportunities to surrender to your fears, but know that you don't have to. The power of mastery is within you, and it gives you the right to pursue victory when defeat seems inevitable. You will never know what is possible for you unless you try. Fear is usually waiting at the back door of the mind, but so are power and love. When we choose to respond to life and its circumstances from an attitude of "I can," the door of possibility opens, and we walk through prepared to do whatever is required to return to a state of wholeness, love, and harmony.

I can't promise you that taking a stand for victory will be easy. It probably won't be easy. But it is possible. If you live from your faith rather than from your fear, you will be closer to victory than if you stand in fear waiting for your worst nightmare to happen. In faith, move forward and know that your God is with you.

Affirmation:

In faith, I move forward with the understanding that the victory is already mine. Thank You, God.

Step Eight

Choose Love

"… love the Lord your God with all your heart, and with all your soul, and with all your mind … You shall love your neighbor as yourself." Matthew 22:37, 39

When asked about the greatest commandment that one can live by, Jesus did not hesitate to say that the greatest commandment is love. First, love the Creator, the One who created you, the One who sustains and maintains you. When you love the Creator, your ability to love will multiply. It will overflow in your life and heal you of your regrets of the past, your fears about the future, and your thoughts and feelings of unworthiness and unforgiveness.

It will also give you the courage to love others–even those whom you believe to be your enemies. You will love them because they, too, are made in the image of God, the Creator.

You won't love them because you approve of their behavior. Oh, no! You will love them because of who they really are as spiritual beings. You will love them because you realize that they are not conscious that every seed they sow they will also reap. You will love them because you cannot afford to harbor thoughts of disappointment, guilt, hate, revenge, anger, fear or shame against them. You love them because if you partner with toxic and negative emotions, there is a consequence that you alone must bear.

You love because you choose to be a habitation of peace, joy, good health, and stable emotions. You love because you do not dare let feelings of unforgiveness rob you of a happy, healthy, and successful life. You love because you are too smart not to. You love because you know that love is sufficient to see you through every adventure of life.

The love that you give returns to you in numerous ways. Right now, make the decision to love God and to trust that you are not alone. Trust that you are being cared for, even if it doesn't appear to be so.

Now, turn that love on yourself. Give yourself permission to be well and strong. Give yourself permission every day in every way to become stronger and stronger. Relax into God's love, and know that your healing is at hand. Feel worthy of this healing, and accept it as a blessing here and now.

Affirmation:

I am worthy! I am worthy of healing. I accept my healing. I am worthy.

Step Nine

Know the Truth

Jesus said, "… know the truth, and the truth will make you free." John 8:32

Your decision to constantly know the spiritual truths stated in this book and other healing works will prove useful to you. Some days you may choose to know and repeat these truths more than other days. One truth may grab your attention more than another. The point is this: Work with whatever works for you. No one knows what touches your soul. Whatever speaks to you in a way that gives you hope and encourages you to be confident of your healing deserves your undivided attention. When you study and embrace the lessons, living true to them, there is a payoff.

A great work is being done within your being. Practice these truths daily in the face of every circumstance. Speak them. Live them to the best of your ability. Pull away from all distractions and know the Truth. The Truth that you know will liberate you and free you to grow forward in grace.

Affirmation:

The truth statements that I affirm in my soul daily have a healing and loving effect in my body and affairs. The Truth has set me free. Praise God!

Step Ten

Be Grateful

*"… give thanks in all circumstances;
for this is the will of God … ."
I Thessalonians 5:18*

A sk your heart for a song, statement, or prayer of gratitude. Choose to be grateful right where you are. Whether you are reading these words or having them read to you, pause right now, and simply be grateful.

Gratitude is an attitude that promotes humble surrender to the present moment. No one knows what the next moment holds, but what we do know is this: In this moment, I can be grateful. I am grateful.

Your constant attitude of gratitude will bless you and will inspire others. When you awaken in the morning, take a few moments to express gratitude for the day. A young woman took the time to speak words of gratitude the night before her surgery. She and her roommate in the hospital simply gave thanks for life. They never asked for the surgery to be cancelled or even postponed. With loving hearts, they gave thanks for the support of family and friends.

The next morning, the young woman was informed by her doctors that the surgery was not necessary. She was discharged from the hospital and sent home to the care of a loving family. Her hospital roommate continued to be grateful. Shortly thereafter, she, too, was discharged from the hospital.

No one can tell you how your exercise in gratitude will bless you, but it will. If you feel tired, be grateful. If you are afraid, be grateful. Wherever you are as you read these words, choose to be grateful, and your gratitude will make its presence known in your life.

Be grateful for all the small miracles that happen every moment. As you give thanks for the small things, the greater things will surely catch your eye and beckon for your attention.

Affirmation:

I am grateful for this moment and all that is unfolding in it. I am safe. I am loved.
I am grateful.

Step Eleven

Rest

"Be still, and know that I am God!"
Psalm 46:10

A well-kept secret is this: Healing requires SILENCE. The healing presence within you operates as you relax and become still. Your stillness allows the healing vibration to exert itself easily and effortlessly.

When you rest, there is calmness, and your body can do what it does naturally — heal. Rest also allows you to hear the whisperings of your inner voice — God's voice. God's will is that you experience wholeness. How can you hear God's message to you if there are no quiet, restful moments?

The best thing that your friends and relatives can do to support you as you heal is to allow you to rest. Numerous visitors and telephone calls may be well meaning, but your ability to be quiet and still will prove more helpful to you than flowers and queries from loved ones.

In the silence, your body is able to regenerate itself. When you conserve your energy, there is more energy to strengthen you. When you are constantly talking, you are dissipating your energy. When you choose to rest, your energy supply is restored rather than depleted.

Resist the temptation to respond to every comment made to you or to enter into conversations that require you to describe your circumstances again and again. Self-control is critical to healing. Let go of feelings and conversations that deplete you, and hold on to the feelings and habits that help you and support you in your healing. If healing is your goal, you must rest.

Affirmation:

I rest in the healing flow of Divine Spirit. I am healed, healed, healed.

Step Twelve

Have Faith

"Have faith in God." Mark 11:22
"faith the size of a mustard seed" Luke 17:6

Have you ever seen a mustard seed? It is very small. You only need faith the size of a mustard seed to see you through your circumstances. You have enough faith because God endowed you with faith when you were created. Now is the time to exercise that faith, to put it to work.

Faith is like a muscle. Its strength is determined by how often you use it. Muscles that are not used often are not as strong as muscles that are flexed daily. Sometimes we appear weak, unable to help ourselves. Appearances are subject to change. When we dare to discover the faith that God gave to us and begin to activate it by cultivating it, or even flexing it, all manner of change can happen for us.

Remember the woman in the Bible who had an issue of blood? For twelve years she relied on her money to address her health issues. It wasn't until her money was depleted that she decided to exercise her faith and risk touching Jesus' garment to claim her healing.

If you've been relying on something or someone for your healing and the desired result has not yet manifested, it is not too late. It is never too late to turn in faith to God who made you and ask for direction. One small act of faith is enough to set your life course in a different direction.

Sure, there are times when we feel helpless, hurt, and just plain tired. But those are the moments that present us with the opportunity to turn to God in prayer. We may not even know what type of help we need. But God does. We may not know how we are going to make it through. But God does. We may feel afraid. But God is our courage. We may feel abandoned. But God is with us. We may not even know how to pray. But God will give us the words or the tears or maybe even the humble heart. You may think you are not worthy of whatever you desire. But God knows that you are worthy. You may be ready to give up, to quit, to end it all. But God has a plan for you, and it is a plan for your good and not for your harm. So don't give up.

Have faith. Have faith that God is with you every step of this journey called life. There has never been a time when God abandoned you, even if it appears that that is exactly what happened. You are stronger than you know, and your faith in the goodness of God is enough, this day, to see you through. Keep going. Trust God to handle the details. Pray for peace, and that peace will be a comfort to you and to those who care for you. Peace has a way of making all things okay. With peace comes strength to endure the challenges, to accept the truth that God, alone, whispers in your heart.

Your faith in God brings peace. You really are okay. No matter what unfolds tomorrow or even today, you are safe. Keep going… Keep growing…Keep being faithful. You won't regret it!

Affirmation:

"My faith in the goodness of God is sufficient to see me through."

My Prayer for You!

Dearest God,

In this moment, I am eternally grateful for Your goodness that abounds this very hour. I affirm life and wholeness for this, Your child. I know that You love this soul with an everlasting love. Your love is more than sufficient to heal, bless, prosper, and free this soul. I boldly affirm healing now! Blessings now! Prosperity now! Freedom now!

With Your amazing grace leading the way, the right circumstances, conditions, professionals, and friends now rush to the aid of this, Your child. All that is needed is provided in a miraculous way. There is total and complete restoration in mind, body, and affairs.

I stand grateful for all that is accomplished in Your name and nature and to Your glory. I place this, Your child, lovingly in Your care and keeping. Guide this soul in the days ahead. I trust that ALL is already well. In Your Name, it is done. Amen.

About the Author

The Reverend Dr. Sheila McKeithen is the spiritual leader of The Universal Centre of Truth for Better Living in Kingston, Jamaica (uctjamaica.org) and is the first elected president of the Universal Foundation for Better Living (ufbl.org). She follows in the footsteps of her spiritual mothers, the Reverend Dr. Johnnie Colemon and the late Reverend Dr. Mary A. Tumpkin, as a proponent of the empowerment message of New Thought Christianity. A clear "mouthpiece" of universal spiritual principles, Rev. Sheila defied the odds in 1986 when her doctors predicted that she had less than six days to live. Nearly 30 years later, Rev. Sheila is alive, alert, enthusiastic, and committed to her mission of serving as a vehicle for hope and healing.

A native of Ft. Lauderdale, Florida, Rev. Sheila was a practicing attorney at the height of her legal career when she received the call to ministry. She relinquished her position as an Assistant Attorney General for the State of Florida in order to minister in Kingston,

Jamaica for what was to be a 6-month assignment. The rest is history! In addition to serving as the spiritual leader of the UFBL ministry in Jamaica, Rev. Sheila also serves as Regional Director for Missions in the Caribbean, the Bahamas and in South America; and as a faculty member for two seminaries: the Johnnie Colemon Theological Seminary in Miami Gardens, FL, and the University of Transformational Studies and Leadership in Culver City, CA. She is the immediate past Southwest Regional Chaplain of Delta Sigma Theta Sorority, Inc.

Rev. Sheila is making her mark within and outside of the New Thought community as a spiritual activist, sought-after speaker, and author: in 2014, she was a featured presenter at Michael Beckwith's Revelation Conference and Jacqueline Atkins' GOLD Rush Women's Conference. She appears in Bishop Vashti McKenzie's book *Those Sisters Can Preach: 22 Pearls of Wisdom, Virtue, and Hope* (2013); and Shajen Joy Aziz and Demian Lichtenstein's documentary book and film *Discover the Gift* (2010). She is also a nine-time author of the monthly UFBL publication, the *Daily Inspiration*, and the producer of a motivational CD titled *Daily Dose of Motivation*. In 2001, Rev. Sheila was inducted into Morehouse College's Martin Luther King, Jr. Board of Preachers.

Made in the USA
San Bernardino, CA
14 April 2016